The Little Book of
Coloring for Calm

100 Mandalas for Relaxation in Minutes

The Little Book of Coloring for Calm

An Hachette UK Company
www.hachette.co.uk

First published in Great Britain in 2015 by
ILEX, a division of Octopus Publishing Group Ltd
Octopus Publishing Group
Carmelite House
50 Victoria Embankment
London, EC4Y 0DZ
www.octopusbooks.co.uk
www.octopusbooksusa.com

Design, layout and text copyright
© Octopus Publishing Group Ltd 2015

Distributed in the US by
Hachette Book Group
1290 Avenue of the Americas
4th and 5th Floors
New York, NY 10020

Distributed in Canada by
Canadian Manda Group
664 Annette St.
Toronto, Ontario, Canada M6S 2C8

PUBLISHER: Roly Allen
COMMISSIONING EDITOR: Zara Larcombe
SENIOR SPECIALIST EDITOR: Frank Gallaugher
SENIOR PROJECT EDITOR: Natalia Price-Cabrera
ASSISTANT EDITOR: Rachel Silverlight
ART DIRECTOR: Julie Weir
DESIGN: Made Noise
SENIOR PRODUCTION MANAGER: Katherine Hockley

Madonna Gauding asserts the moral right to be
identified as the author of this work

ISBN 978-1-78157-314-3

A CIP catalogue record for this book is available
from the British Library

Printed and bound in China

10 9 8 7 6 5 4 3

The Little Book of
Coloring for Calm

100 Mandalas for Relaxation in Minutes

Madonna Gauding

WHAT IS A MANDALA?

A mandala is a sacred circle, a symbol of wholeness. The word "mandala" comes from the Sanskrit word meaning "circle" or "sacred center"; although the word has its origins in ancient India, this sacred symbol is found in all cultures, expressed in art, architecture, and everyday objects. Mandalas are usually circular in form (although they can sometimes appear as circles or triangles within squares), and they are always symmetrical, drawing your eye toward their central element.

WHY COLOR MANDALAS?

Mandala coloring is an enjoyable pastime, but its benefits go far beyond having fun. Coloring intricate designs demands mental focus and concentration, similar to the concentration you can develop during meditation. This focus naturally causes you to suspend your mental chatter, achieving a kind of mindfulness that will leave you refreshed, calm, and focused.

DE-STRESS

The designs in this book have been created with relaxation in mind, and their small size means that you will quickly feel the benefit of the coloring process; within just a few minutes you should find yourself absorbed in the flow of bringing a beautiful design slowly to life. You can take this book anywhere you like—think of it as an emergency de-stressing kit!

MATERIALS & TECHNIQUES

Colored pencils are ideal, or you could try using watercolors, acrylics, felt-tipped pens, or markers. Paints or liquid inks may cause the paper to wrinkle; to prevent this, place blotting paper above and below the completed mandala, and a weight on top, then leave the paper undisturbed until it dries flat. If you are coloring with pencils, keep erasers and smudge tools handy, including a piece of leather chamois for shading. Shading from light to dark within segments of the mandala can create a subtle, three-dimensional effect; solid colors appear more jewel-like and, if chosen well, can also provide a sense of dimension and depth.

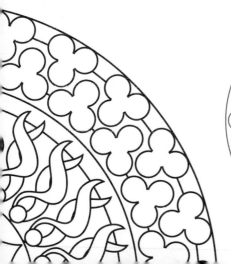

FEEL THE BENEFITS!

Of course, you don't have to do more than simply enjoy the process of coloring the designs in this book. However, if you want to enhance your experience, try focusing on a specific problem or issue – anything that might be making you feel tense, stressed, or anxious – as you color. Give your unconscious mind "instructions" in the form of a question, and then just relax and enjoy the process.

As you color, you may discover solutions to problems that you previously considered intractable. Here are three ways that you can benefit from mandala coloring, particularly suited to the small designs in this book...

TO RELAX

Before you begin, ask yourself what you might do to change your life so that you have less stress and anxiety.

Color your mandala any way you like. When you have finished, write down ten ways in which you might relieve stress in your life. Be creative and don't censor what you write.

Select three suggestions from your list and commit to making those changes within the next month.

TO INSPIRE CREATIVITY

Choose a mandala with a design that appeals to your visual sense.

Trace its lines with your finger, enjoying the pattern of repeating motifs, and use colours that delight your senses. Experiment with patterns and shading, using alternating patches of light and dark hues.

When you have finished, write down your insights on being more creative in your approach to everyday tasks.

TO SOLVE A PROBLEM

Bring to mind a current problem that is especially difficult or worrisome. Write down your concern as best you can, including two possible solutions.

Choose a mandala that you intuitively feel holds a solution to your problem. If you don't get a "vibe" from any of the mandalas, simply pick one that attracts you at this moment.

When you have completed the design, write down any thoughts or images that arose while you were coloring. Examine the shades you chose: do they hold any clues? Now bring to mind your problem once again and generate a third solution.

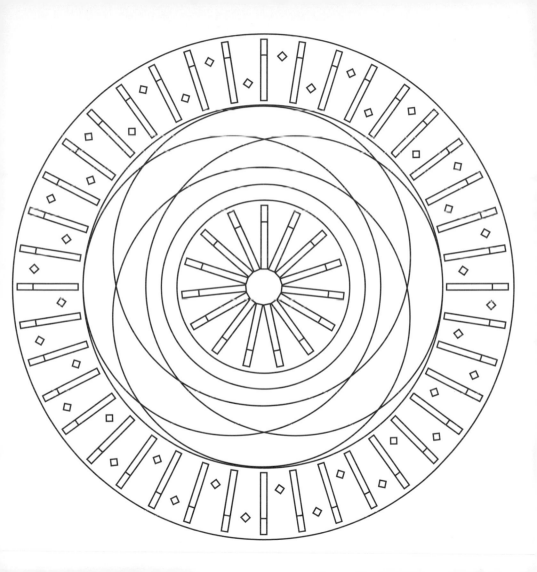

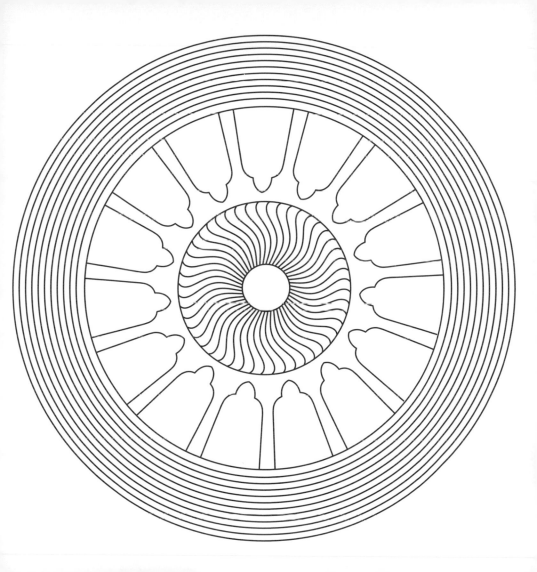

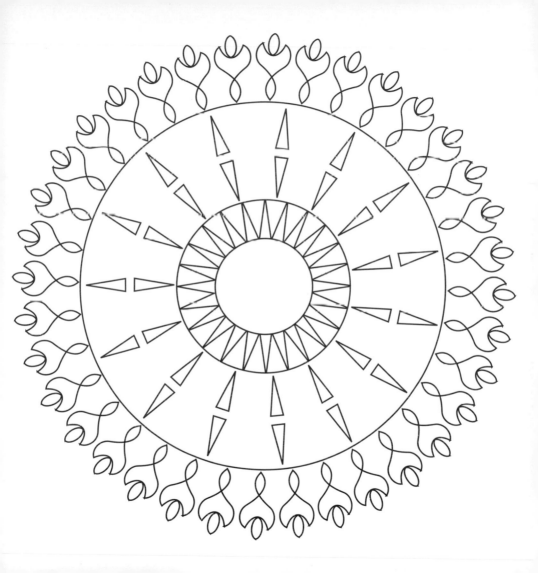

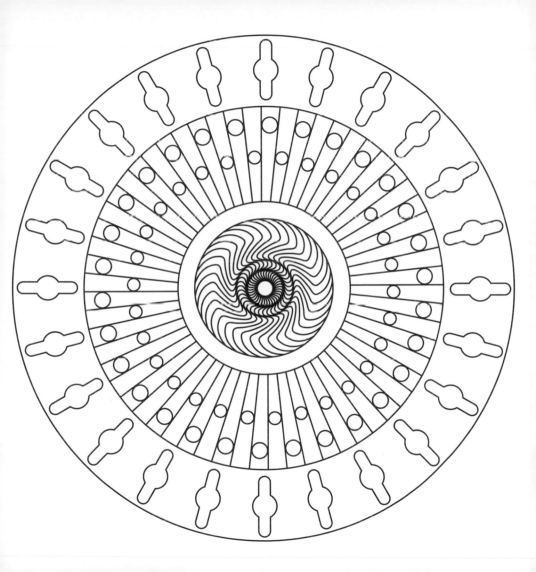

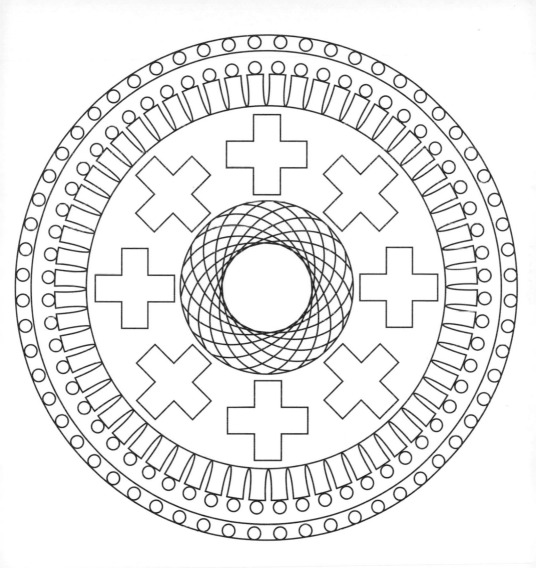